COOKING SKILLS

VEGETARIAN FOOD

CLAUDIA MARTIN

Enslow Publishing
101 W. 23rd Street
Suite 240
New York, NY 10011
USA
enslow.com

Published in 2019 by Enslow Publishing, LLC.
101 W. 23rd Street, Suite 240, New York, NY 10011

Copyright © 2019 Enslow Publishing, LLC

All rights reserved.

Editors: Sarah Eason and Jennifer Sanderson
Designers: Paul Myerscough and Simon Borrough
Picture Researcher: Claudia Martin

No part of this book may be reproduced by any means without the written permission of the publisher.

Cataloging-in-Publication Data
Names: Martin, Claudia.
Title: Vegetarian food / Claudia Martin.
Description: New York : Enslow Publishing, 2019. | Series: Cooking skills | Includes glossary and index.
Identifiers: ISBN 9781978506688 (pbk.) | ISBN 9781978506411 (library bound) | ISBN 9781978506350 (ebook)
Subjects: LCSH: Vegetarian cooking—Juvenile literature. | Cookbooks—Juvenile literature.
Classification: LCC TX837.M35 2019 | DDC 641.5'636—dc23

Printed in the United States of America

To Our Readers: We have done our best to make sure all website addresses in this book were active and appropriate when we went to press. However, the author and the publisher have no control over and assume no liability for the material available on those websites or on any websites they may link to. Any comments or suggestions can be sent by e-mail to customerservice@enslow.com.

Photo Credits: Cover: Shutterstock: AS Food Studio: tc; Jan H Andersen: bl; Monkey Business Images: br; misuma: bc. Inside: Shutterstock: Africa Studio: pp.13c, 17, 29; ahturner: p.41b; Alastair Wallace: pp.14–15; Alliance: pp.10–11; Andrey_Popov: p.15b; Angel Simon: p.36t; Artem Shadrin: p.43c; AS Food Studio: p.24–25; AshTproductions: p.26cl; Bukhta Ihor: p.25; carpaumar: pp.20–21; chris kolaczan: p.31b; Dean Drobot: p.37; Elizabeth Foster: pp.18b, 45r; El Nariz: p.24; Enlightened Media: p.36b; Eugenia Lucasenco: p.34l; Filimages: pp.2–3, 21t, 46–47, 48; Foxys Forest Manufacture: p.34c; from my point of view: pp.38–39; GCapture: p.11; Haurashko Kseniya: pp.22–23; hiphoto: pp.32–33; Iakov Filimonov: p.34r; I Am Nikom: pp.32b, 46; ittoilmatar: p.19; Jan H Andersen: p.21c; jeehyun: p.26tr; joannawnuk: p.38; JP Wallet: p.9; Julia Wave: p.22b; Koy Jung: p.33; kuvona: pp.30–31, 36–37; LADO: pp.1b, 6–7, 13t; Magrig: pp.12–13; Malykalexa: p.13b; marco mayer: p.21b; margouillat photo: p.22t; maroke: p.30; michaeljung: p.39b; Miracle Stock: p.28; Monkey Business Images: p.11b; mubus7: p.41t; NaughtyNut: p.16; nenetus: pp.8–9; oBebee: pp.16–17; October22: p.32t; Olya Detry: p.39t; oneinchpunch: p.44; osoznanie.jizni: p.5t; Peter Zijlstra: pp.1t, 18t; Photographee. eu: p.5b; Plateresca: pp.34–35; Rimma Bondarenko: pp.40–41; Robyn Mackenzie: pp.43b, 44–45; rukxstockphoto: p.31t; Ryco Montefont: p.45l; Sea Wave: pp.42–43; Sergey Yechikov: pp.26–27; sirikorn thamniyom: pp.28–29; Solomiya Malovana: p.43t; stockcreations: pp.4–5; teleginatania: pp.18–19; Victoria Shuba: p.15t.

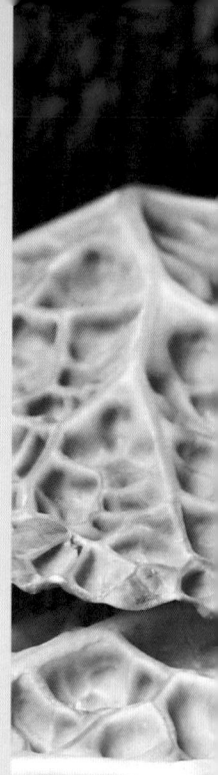

CONTENTS

Chapter 1 Get Cooking! — 4
   Read the Recipe… — 6
   …Or Go Your Own Way — 8

Chapter 2 Voting for Veg — 10
   Stuffed Bell Peppers — 12
   Cauliflower and Cheese — 14

Chapter 3 Packing in Protein — 16
   Mushroom Stroganoff — 18
   Bean Hotpot — 20

Chapter 4 Taking to Tofu — 22
   Chinese Stir–Fry — 24
   Tofu Kebabs — 26

Chapter 5 Rocking Rice — 28
   Risotto al Pomodoro — 30
   Egg-Fried Rice — 32

Chapter 6 Getting into Grains — 34
   Spiced Couscous — 36
   Tabbouleh — 38

Chapter 7 Pepping up Potatoes — 40
   Dauphinoise Potatoes — 42
   Spicy Potato Wedges — 44

Glossary — 46
Further Reading — 47
Index — 48

CHAPTER 1
GET COOKING!

Whether you are vegetarian yourself or you enjoy entertaining friends who are, cooking vegetarian food can be fun, giving you tasty, healthy, and exciting results.

A Vegetarian Diet

Vegetarian recipes do not contain any meat, poultry, or fish, or any products made from them. But what are the bonuses to eating vegetarian food? Some people are vegetarian because they believe it is a compassionate choice. Others are vegetarian because it can be a healthy choice. The best vegetarian dishes contain plenty of whole grains, plant-based proteins, fruits, and vegetables.

Since a vegetarian diet is low in animal fats—it is not free from them unless you are vegan—it is also low in saturated fat, the "bad" fat that can lead to heart disease.

Eating for Health

Vegetarian teens need to be sure that they eat enough protein to fuel growth and activity. Vegetarian protein comes in the form of beans, legumes, nuts, tofu, and mushrooms.

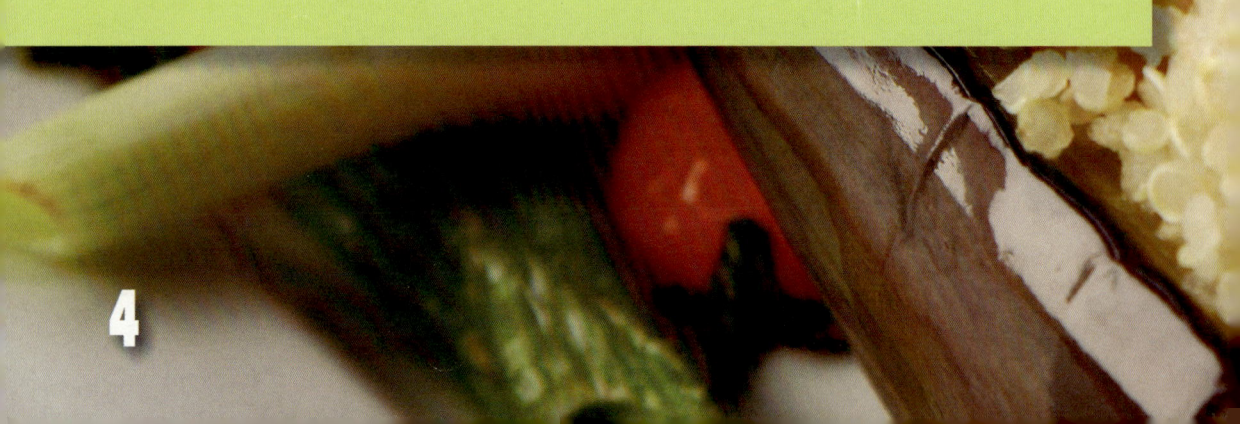

They also need to ensure they do not miss out on iron (found in dried beans, spinach, and iron-fortified breakfast cereals), calcium (in dairy products, leafy greens, tofu, and beans), vitamin B12 (in eggs and dairy products), and vitamin D (in dairy products).

Dietary Requirements

Before planning a meal for friends, find out if they have any special dietary needs, such as a wheat or gluten intolerance or allergy. Gluten-free alternatives can be found in many grocery stores and health-food stores.

mixed spices

Store It Up

If you keep a selection of basic ingredients in your pantry or refrigerator, you will always be able to cook up a delicious and healthy vegetarian meal in minutes. Start off with these staple ingredients:

- Whole grains
- Canned beans
- Tofu
- Vegetarian cheese
- Vegetable oil
- Canned tomatoes
- Dried herbs and spices
- Selection of fresh vegetables

READ THE RECIPE...

So where do you start? The first thing to do is choose a recipe that you and your friends will enjoy.

Plan Your Meal

The recipes in this book are divided into food groups to help you plan your meals. We start off with recipes that have vegetables as the star of the show (Chapter 2), then move onto vegetarian proteins (Chapter 3) and tasty tofu (Chapter 4). The second half of the book is based on carbohydrates: rice (Chapter 5), more unusual grains (Chapter 6), and potatoes (Chapter 7). If you are cooking for vegans, choose a recipe that does not contain milk products or eggs (see pages 24, 26, 36, 38, and 44), or cook a different recipe but switch out those ingredients.

Gather Your Ingredients

Once you have chosen a recipe, check out the ingredients you will need. Each of the recipes serves four people, so multiply or divide as needed. Make a list of any missing ingredients, then head to the store. Make sure you read the labels to find vegetarian cheese (without rennet) and, if you have animal-welfare concerns, look for free-range eggs. There are vegan alternatives for almost anything—how about trying vegan cheese and sour cream?

Time It Right

So, you have invited friends over for the evening, but when do you start cooking? Always overestimate how long it will take, so you do not feel rushed while you are still draining the tofu. Read the recipe instructions carefully. The ingredients are listed in the order they are used, to make sure you do not leave out any of them. If you do not feel confident about your cooking skills, look at the "Mastering the Basics" sections at the start of each chapter.

How Much, How Hot?

In these recipes, measurements are given in ounces (oz), followed by grams (g), as well as cups, followed by milliliters (ml) or liters (l). There are 240 ml in each cup. Sometimes, you will need to add a teaspoon (tsp) or tablespoon (tbsp) of an ingredient. There are 5 ml in each teaspoon and 15 ml in each tablespoon. When a "handful" or a "pinch" is suggested, the exact quantity is less important—add more or less for a stronger or weaker taste.

Oven temperatures are given in degrees Fahrenheit (°F), followed by degrees Celsius (°C). If you are not sure how hot to have the stove, start low then adjust upward—it is better to cook slowly than to burn!

...OR GO YOUR OWN WAY

If you like, you can just use the recipes in this book as guidelines, then let your inner chef go wild!

Taste and See

The first time you cook one of the recipes, you can play it safe by following the instructions closely. While you are enjoying the results, think about what you like and dislike about the flavors and textures. Would you prefer more of the goat's cheese but less of the cayenne? Do you hate the texture of bulgur wheat but love the mint leaves? Could the recipe do with an extra dose of excitement, like crunchy croutons or a sprinkling of chili?

Tips and Switches

The "Chef's Tip" box alongside each recipe might give you some ideas for adding different, richer, or spicier flavors. Also have a look at the "Switch It Up" boxes on the first page of each chapter, which give yet more ideas for changing ingredients. But as you develop as a chef, you will come up with plenty more ideas of your own!

Swapping Sides!

Another way to make changes is to swap the carbohydrates. If the recipe suggests rice, try couscous, bulgur wheat, noodles, or pasta instead. Do not forget breads, such as corn bread, naan, or tortillas. Remember though: all carbohydrates are not created equally. Whenever possible, opt for whole grains, which have not been processed to remove the fiber and nutrient-rich germ (kernel) and bran (outer layer).

Keep It Clean

Hygiene is very important in any kitchen. Before you cook:

- Wash your hands with soap and warm water.
- Make sure all your work surfaces and equipment are clean.
- Use a different cutting board from the one that anyone in the family uses for raw meat or fish.
- If you have long hair, tie it back.
- Wash fruit and vegetables under cold running water.
- Check the use-by dates on your ingredients.
- Do not leave food out of the refrigerator for longer than two hours.

CHAPTER 2
VOTING FOR VEG

Cook your vegetables just right: tender, but not so soft that they lose their flavor and goodness.

Cook Like a Chef!

There are many methods of cooking vegetables, including boiling, stir-frying (also called sautéing), roasting, stewing, and broiling. Boiling (used in "Cauliflower and Cheese" on page 14) is quick and simple, but over-boiled vegetables will be mushy, tasteless, and low in nutrients. Stir-frying (used in "Stuffed Bell Peppers" on page 12 to cook the onions) leaves vegetables full of flavor and texture. When stir-frying, check the heat and stir to prevent burning. Roasting (used for the "Stuffed Bell Peppers") is a slower method, leaving vegetables with a deeper and sweeter flavor. Stewing (used in "Bean Hotpot" on page 20) is when vegetables are simmered in sauce, locking in more flavor and nutrients than boiling in water. Finally, grilling (used in "Tofu Kebabs" on page 26) is great for texture, as long as you turn your vegetables to prevent charring.

Mastering the Basics
Chopping Onions

Onions are often added to recipes to give flavor, aroma, and texture. An important skill is peeling and chopping onions quickly and safely. The less time you spend over your onions, the fewer tears you will cry! Here is how:

1. Place the onion on a cutting board. Cut off the top of the onion (the opposite end from the roots) to give you a base.
2. Rest the onion on its base, then slice it in half vertically, cutting down through the roots. Peel off the skin.
3. Put one half of the onion on its flat side. Holding at the root end and keeping your fingers clear of the knife, make five or six parallel, vertical cuts down through the onion, with the tip of your knife pointing toward the root. Leave the section close to the root untouched so your onion does not yet fall apart.
4. Now rotate your onion. Slice down through the onion horizontally, so you have made crisscross cuts—your diced pieces of onion should fall away as you go! Discard the root.
5. Repeat with the other half.

Switch It Up

If you enjoy the Stuffed Bell Peppers on page 12, try stuffing and baking eggplants or large tomatoes. Do not discard the insides of these vegetables—just add them to your filling when you fry it. You do not need to boil eggplants and tomatoes before baking, but increase the baking time for eggplants to at least thirty minutes and to twenty minutes for tomatoes.

STUFFED BELL PEPPERS

This tasty recipe will leave you and your friends feeling nicely stuffed!

You Will Need
7 oz (200 g) rice
4 red bell peppers
1 tbsp olive oil
1 medium onion, peeled and chopped
15 oz (425 g) can of chopped tomatoes
Salt and pepper
7 oz (200 g) vegetarian goat's cheese, sliced
Handful of black olives to garnish

Instructions
1. Preheat the oven to 390°F (200°C).
2. Cook the rice in boiling water for ten to twelve minutes.
3. While the rice is cooking, cut the tops off the bell peppers, then scoop out the seeds and pith. Cook the bell peppers in a large pan of boiling water for seven minutes. Set them aside.
4. Heat the olive oil in a frying pan and cook the onion over a low heat until softened.
5. Add the tomatoes to the onion, season to taste, then bring to a simmer.
6. When the rice is cooked and drained, stir in the tomato and onion sauce.
7. Put the bell peppers on a baking sheet, spoon in the tomato rice, then top with goat's cheese.
8. Bake for ten minutes, then garnish with the olives.

The olives add flavor and interest to this tasty meal.

CHEF'S TIP
To up the protein count, add 3 oz (85 g) of mushrooms to your filling. Just fry them with the onions.

goat's cheese

13

CAULIFLOWER AND CHEESE

A classic crowd-pleaser, serve this cauliflower and cheese with some wholegrain bread and salad.

You Will Need
1 large cauliflower
2 oz (55 g) butter
4 tbsp all-purpose flour
2½ cups (600 ml) milk
4 oz (115 g) cheddar cheese, grated
Salt and pepper

Instructions
1. Preheat the oven to 390°F (200°C).
2. Cut the cauliflower into bite-size florets (the flower-like heads), discarding the thickest stalks. Cook in a large saucepan of boiling water for five to six minutes. Place the drained florets in an ovenproof dish.
3. In a saucepan, melt the butter, then stir in the flour. Continue stirring, over a low heat, for two minutes.
4. Stirring constantly, add the milk a splash at a time. Simmer for five minutes, stirring frequently. Season to taste.
5. Remove the pan from the heat, then mix in most of the cheese. Pour the sauce over the cauliflower, then sprinkle the remaining cheese.
6. Bake for ten minutes until the top is golden.

Cauliflower and cheese makes a great weekday meal.

CHEF'S TIP
For an even more flavorful sauce, try adding 1 tsp of English mustard.

CHAPTER 3
PACKING IN PROTEIN

Even when meat and fish are off the list, there are many delicious protein sources to choose from.

Powered by Protein

Protein is essential for repairing all the body's cells and for building new ones in brains, muscles, tissues, and bones. The average teen needs about 1.8 oz (51 g) of protein per day. So what are the best ways to pack that in?

Start with legumes and pulses: lentils and beans, from cannellini beans to black beans and chickpeas, are great sources of protein. Soybeans make their way onto this list, too, along with the products made from them, such as soy milk, tofu, and tempeh. Some whole grains have a decent amount of protein, including oats and barley. Nuts and seeds are an easy-to-snack-on form of protein, with almonds, cashews, and chia seeds very good sources. Quinoa (pronounced "keen-wa"), technically a seed but eaten like a grain, is high in protein. If you eat dairy products and eggs, these are rich in protein, with one egg containing 0.2 oz (6 g).

Mastering the Basics
Thickening Sauces

Both the recipes in this chapter are cooked in a sauce. Knowing how to thicken a sauce when it is too runny and watery is a vital skill. One method is to use a basic pantry ingredient—all-purpose flour. Flour contains starch molecules that bond with water when heated, creating a gel. Here is how to do it:

1. In a mug, mix together 1 tbsp cold water with 1 tbsp all-purpose flour. This will be enough to thicken a small quantity of sauce. Increase your quantities to 4 tbsp each of water and flour to thicken a family soup.
2. When smooth, stir this flour slurry into your hot sauce.
3. Bring your sauce to a simmer for five minutes and watch your sauce thicken as it simmers.

Switch It Up

Each portion of the Mushroom Stroganoff on page 18 contains about 0.2 oz (6 g) of protein. That is roughly 0.16 oz (4.75 g) in the mushrooms, 0.03 oz (1 g) in the sour cream, and a tiny 0.01 oz (0.25 g) in the onion. To bump up the protein, try stirring 1 tbsp chia seeds into each portion, adding 0.07 oz (2 g) of protein. How about serving it with quinoa, offering another 0.14 oz (4 g) of protein per plate?

17

MUSHROOM STROGANOFF

Stroganoff is a Russian recipe, made with sour cream—it is great on a cold winter's night.

paprika

A perfect combination of creamy sauce and juicy mushrooms!

You Will Need
- 1 tbsp olive oil
- 1 medium onion, chopped
- 1 tbsp paprika
- 2 garlic cloves, chopped
- 1 lb 5 oz (600 g) mixed mushrooms, sliced
- 1¼ cups (300 ml) vegetable stock
- 6 tbsp sour cream
- Salt and pepper
- Sage leaves to garnish (optional)

Instructions
1. Heat the olive oil in a large, thick-bottomed frying pan, then cook the onion for about five minutes, until softened.
2. Add the paprika, garlic, and mushrooms. Cook for five or six minutes, stirring frequently.
3. Pour in the stock, then bring to the boil. Simmer for five minutes until the sauce thickens.
4. Remove the pan from the heat, then stir through the sour cream. Season to taste.
5. If you like, garnish your plates with sage leaves.

CHEF'S TIP
Stir through a small handful of chopped parsley to add a little color and a fresher taste.

BEAN HOTPOT

It takes less than twenty minutes to rustle up this super-easy, protein-packed stew.

You Will Need
- 1 tbsp olive oil
- 1 large onion, chopped
- 2 medium carrots, chopped
- 3 garlic cloves, chopped
- 1 cup (240 ml) vegetable stock
- 15 oz (425 g) can of chopped tomatoes
- 15 oz (425 g) can of cannellini or kidney beans
- Handful of green cabbage, sliced
- 1½ oz (45 g) Italian-style vegetarian cheese, grated
- Salt and pepper

Instructions
1. Heat the oil in a large saucepan, then fry the onions, carrots, and garlic until soft.
2. Pour in the stock, tomatoes, beans, and cabbage, then bring to the boil. Reduce the heat and simmer for around eight minutes until the vegetables are tender.
3. Stir in the cheese, then season with salt and pepper to taste.

This recipe is one big bowl of comfort!

CHEF'S TIP
You can adjust the quantity of stock to give more or less of a soupy consistency to your hotpot.

cannellini beans

21

CHAPTER 4
TAKING TO TOFU

Tofu, sometimes called "bean curd," is made from soy milk. This means it is full of protein and iron.

Making Tofu

Soy milk is made from soaked, ground, and boiled soybeans. To produce tofu, the milk has to be coagulated, or curdled, which means it is turned into a semi-solid by a chemical reaction with salts or acidic substances. The curds are pressed into soft, white blocks.

Terrific Tofu

Tofu has a subtle flavor, so it can be used in both savory and sweet recipes, where it will take on the flavors of the spices or other flavorings. Make sure you pick the right type of tofu for your purposes. The recipes in this chapter use "firm" tofu, which keeps its shape when cooked, making it perfect for stir-fries, curries, grilling, and baking. "Medium firm" tofu is crumblier, so could be mixed in with vegetables in a recipe where they are stuffed. "Soft" or "silken" tofu is creamy, making it ideal for stirring into smoothies, sauces, and desserts.

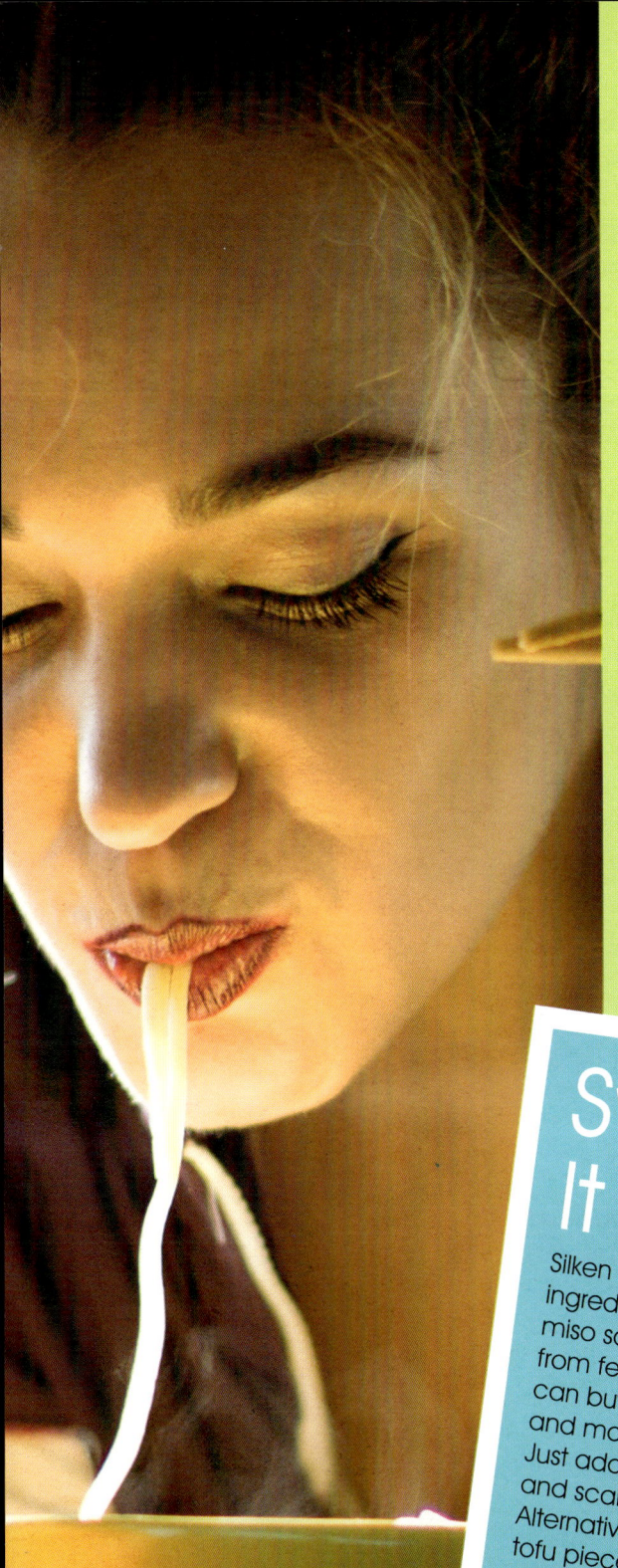

Mastering the Basics
Pressing Tofu

Most tofu is sold packed in water. If a recipe calls for "firm" tofu, one of the best skills to master is pressing tofu to make it firmer. A waterlogged piece of tofu will not absorb a marinade or become crispy in a wok or frying pan. Here is how to do it:

1. Remove the tofu from its packaging. Slice it no more than 1 inch (2.5 cm) thick.
2. Wrap the tofu in layers of paper towel.
3. Place the wrapped tofu between two cutting boards, then weigh down the top board with a heavy pan.
4. Let the tofu sit for at least one hour—the longer, the better.

Switch It Up

Silken tofu is one of the main ingredients in delicious Japanese miso soup. Miso stock is made from fermented soybeans. You can buy it from Asian groceries and many large supermarkets. Just add bite-sized pieces of tofu and scallions, then heat through. Alternatively, you could add silken tofu pieces to any vegetable broth or store-bought soup.

CHINESE STIR-FRY

This recipe tastes as good as a takeout, without having to dial that number.

You Will Need
- 2 tbsp sesame oil
- 10 oz (285 g) firm tofu, pressed and cut into 1-inch (2.5 cm) cubes
- 1 medium onion, chopped
- 5 oz (140 g) mushrooms, chopped
- 5 oz (140 g) broccoli, cut into florets
- 1 garlic clove, peeled and crushed
- 1 inch (2.5 cm) piece of fresh ginger, cut into slivers
- 3 tbsp soy sauce
- 3 tbsp sesame seeds

Instructions
1. Heat 1 tbsp of sesame oil in a large frying pan. Cook the tofu for one to two minutes on each side until golden. Transfer the tofu to a plate.
2. Add a little more sesame oil to the pan if needed, add the onion, and stir-fry for five minutes.
3. Add the mushrooms, broccoli, garlic, and ginger, then stir-fry for another five minutes.
4. Add in the tofu, soy sauce, and sesame seeds, then stir-fry until heated through.

Serve on a nest of noodles or a pile of rice.

CHEF'S TIP
If your stir-fry dries out, add an extra splash of soy sauce and a dash of water.

TOFU KEBABS

Invite your friends over to impress them with these tempting kebabs.

Straight off the grill and into your photo gallery!

26

You Will Need

1 large red onion, chopped into large pieces
1 bell pepper, chopped into large pieces
1 medium zucchini, chopped into large pieces
5 oz (140 g) button mushrooms
10 oz (285 g) firm tofu, cut into 1-inch (2.5-cm) cubes
2 tbsp hoisin sauce
1 tsp soy sauce
2 tsp canola oil
1 tsp lime juice

Instructions

1. Thread pieces of onion, bell pepper, zucchini, mushroom, and tofu onto skewers.
2. To make the marinade, mix the hoisin, soy sauce, oil, and lime juice in a bowl.
3. Brush (or drizzle with a spoon) about half the marinade over the skewers.
4. Heat the barbecue grill or broiler to a medium temperature.
5. Barbecue or broil the skewers for six to seven minutes.
6. Turn over the skewers and brush with the rest of the marinade.
7. Barbecue or broil for another six to seven minutes or until the tofu is golden and the vegetables are tender.

CHEF'S TIP

For a deeper flavor, marinate your tofu and vegetables for thirty minutes.

CHAPTER 5
ROCKING RICE

Around the world, rice is a staple food, but that does not mean it has to be boring.

Types of Rice

Did you know that there are many different types of rice? For a start, there is white rice and brown, or whole grain, rice. Both contain plenty of energy-giving carbohydrates, but brown rice is also full of fiber and nutrients. The carbohydrate from whole grains is absorbed more slowly into your bloodstream, which helps keeps your energy levels stable.

There are also long-, medium-, and short-grained rice. Long-grained types, such as basmati and most store-bought varieties, keep their shape after cooking. Medium-grained varieties, such as arborio and carnaroli, break down a little while cooking, so they are used in Italian risottos and Spanish paella. Short-grained types are used for mushy desserts like rice pudding.

Mastering the Basics
Cooking Rice

Cooking rice seems like the easiest task in the world—until you end up with crunchy grit or a sloppy mess. Different varieties of rice need different cooking times (check the packaging), but in general the following steps will serve up fluffy grains:

1. Most varieties of rice are best when rinsed before cooking. Pour the rice, about ½ cup (90 g) per person, into a strainer and hold under cold running water.
2. Fill a large saucepan with water, add a teaspoon of salt, then bring to a boil.
3. Pour in the rice. Stir immediately but not again, because stirring makes rice sticky.
4. Bring the water back to a boil, then reduce the heat so the water is bubbling steadily but not vigorously.
5. Leave the rice to boil, with no lid covering the pan, for ten minutes—or longer, depending on the variety.
6. To check if the rice is cooked, lift out a few grains with a slotted spoon, let them cool, then taste. If the grains are crunchy, leave for another minute, then try again.
7. Drain the rice into a large strainer—to avoid scalding, balance the strainer inside a colander in the sink.
8. Rinse the rice by pouring very hot water over it. Leave to drain well, then serve.

Switch It Up

Once you know how to make a basic risotto (see page 30), you can cook up any kind you like. How about making a pea risotto by throwing in 3 oz (85 g) frozen peas five minutes before the end, along with the juice of half a lemon? Or try frying 8 oz (225 g) chopped zucchini, then mixing it into the finished risotto?

RISOTTO AL POMODORO

Once you have mastered this rich tomato rice, you will want to cook it again and again.

You Will Need
4 cups (960 ml) vegetable stock
1 oz (30 g) butter
3 tbsp olive oil
2 shallots, finely chopped
2 garlic cloves, peeled and crushed
1¼ cups (250 g) risotto rice
15 oz (425 g) can of chopped tomatoes
Handful of cherry tomatoes, quartered
1 oz (30 g) cheddar cheese, grated

Instructions
1. Heat the vegetable stock and leave to simmer.
2. Heat the butter and olive oil in a large, thick-bottomed saucepan. Add the shallots and fry gently for four to five minutes.
3. Add the garlic and fry for another two minutes.
4. Stir the rice into the oily mixture. Cook for three to four minutes until the grains of rice turn slightly see-through.
5. Add the can of tomatoes and one ladle of hot vegetable stock. Stir regularly until all the stock is absorbed, then add another ladle of stock, stirring frequently until all that liquid is absorbed.
6. Continue stirring and adding stock until all the stock is used up and the rice is soft but not mushy. Depending on the type of rice, this could take thirty to forty minutes from the moment you first added liquid.
7. Serve while piping hot, garnished with cherry tomatoes and cheese.

CHEF'S TIP
Make sure you use risotto rice (often called "arborio") rather than ordinary rice—ordinary rice is not starchy enough.

EGG-FRIED RICE

Serve this fragrant rice as a quick lunch or alongside a stir-fry.

Quick, easy—and especially delicious!

You Will Need
- 2 cups (360 g) long-grain rice
- 2 eggs
- 2 tbsp vegetable oil
- 1 bunch of scallions, chopped
- 2 tbsp soy sauce
- 2 tsp sesame oil

Instructions
1. Cook the rice according to the package instructions (see page 29). Drain it, then set aside.
2. Crack the eggs into a small mixing bowl, then beat with a whisk or fork.
3. Heat the vegetable oil in a large frying pan or wok. Add the scallions and stir-fry over a high heat for one minute.
4. Add the rice, then mix well.
5. Make a hole, or "well," in the center of the rice and pour in the eggs. When the bottom of the eggs starts to set, stir to scramble them. When completely scrambled, stir through the rice.
6. Stir in the soy sauce and sesame oil, then serve.

CHEF'S TIP
For an extra dose of fiber and protein, add 4 oz (115 g) of frozen peas just after the scallions.

CHAPTER 6
GETTING INTO GRAINS

Grains are where we get most of our energy, so make them as exciting as possible by switching them around and spicing them up!

Grains Are Good

Grains are small, hard seeds that can be stored for a long time without refrigeration, which is why they are staple foods around the world. Some grains, such as wheat, are often milled into flour; some, such as canola, are commonly pressed for oil; while others, such as rice, are usually cooked and eaten in their natural form.

Common table grains include barley (in bread and soups), maize (in cornflakes), oats (in oatmeal), rice, and wheat (in bread, pasta, and baked goods). Some more unusual grain products are showcased in the recipes in this chapter. North African couscous is tiny balls of durum wheat, a very hard variety of the grain. Bulgur wheat, traditionally from the Middle East, is the kernels of durum wheat.

Mastering the Basics
Cooking Couscous

Couscous, particularly when whole grain, is a healthy alternative to rice. Couscous must be carefully steamed rather than boiled. Here is how to master perfect couscous:

1. Allow about ½ cup (100 g) dried couscous per person; less if you are making a side dish. For each 1 cup (200 g) of couscous, use 1½ cups (360 ml) of water.
2. In a pan, bring the water to a boil. Add ½ tsp salt and 1 tsp butter to the water.
3. Pour your couscous into the boiling water, stir once, then cover the pan with a lid and remove from the heat.
4. Let the couscous steam for five minutes (or the time recommended on the package), without lifting the lid.
5. After five minutes, check that all the water is absorbed. If not, leave a little longer. Test your couscous: if it tastes too grainy, add a splash more water.
6. Couscous tends to stick together, so fluff with a fork before serving.

Switch It Up

If you would like to be more experimental with your grains, try polenta, a dish of boiled and mushed cornmeal from Italy. If you like your bread, how about eating the Indian flatbread bhakri, made from pearl millet? Or try a German pumpernickel, made from rye, or a spelt roll, called a dinkelbrot.

SPICED COUSCOUS

There are a lot of spices in this recipe, making it mouth-wateringly delicious.

cumin

36

The spices in this dish taste and smell great.

You Will Need
- 1 tbsp vegetable oil
- 2 scallions, chopped
- 1 garlic clove, sliced
- 1 bell pepper, chopped
- 4 large tomatoes, chopped
- 1 medium zucchini, chopped
- 1 large carrot, peeled and chopped
- Pinch of salt
- 1 tsp ground cumin
- ½ tsp ground ginger
- ¼ tsp ground cinnamon
- ¼ tsp cayenne pepper
- 2 cups (400 g) dry couscous
- 3 cups (720 ml) water
- Sprig of basil to garnish (optional)

Instructions
1. Heat the oil in a frying pan, then add the scallions, garlic, bell pepper, tomatoes, zucchini, and carrot. Stir-fry for five minutes, then set aside.
2. Put the salt, cumin, ginger, cinnamon, and cayenne pepper in a mixing bowl.
3. In a large saucepan, bring the water to a boil. Stir in the couscous and mixed spices, then remove from the heat and cover. Leave to steam for five minutes, until the water is absorbed.
4. Mix the vegetables into the couscous, then serve, garnished with basil.

CHEF'S TIP
Instead of frying the vegetables, try tossing them in 3 tbsp of olive oil and roasting in the oven at 390°F (200°C) for twenty to twenty-five minutes.

TABBOULEH

Serve this traditional Middle Eastern bulgur wheat salad as a side dish to impress your friends.

You Will Need
¾ cup (170 g) bulgur wheat, rinsed
About 2 cups (480 ml) boiling water
3 cups (180 g) flat-leaf parsley leaves, chopped
1 cup (60 g) fresh mint leaves, chopped
3 large tomatoes, chopped
1 small onion, finely chopped
2 tbsp olive oil
⅓ cup (80 ml) lemon juice
Salt and pepper

Instructions
1. Pour the bulgur wheat into a bowl, then cover with boiling water. Leave for twenty to twenty-five minutes or until it is soft.
2. Over the sink, tip the bulgur wheat into a large strainer to drain.
3. Rinse the bulgur wheat in cold running water, then drain again. Press with a spoon to squeeze out any remaining water. Put the bulgur wheat into a large bowl.
4. Add the parsley, mint, tomatoes, and onion to the bulgur wheat.
5. To make a dressing, pour the olive oil and lemon juice into a container, then whisk with a fork. Pour over the bulgur wheat.
6. Season with salt and pepper, then chill in the refrigerator for at least an hour before serving.

Get ready to wake up your taste buds.

CHEF'S TIP

For an even more colorful plate, add the seeds from a pomegranate—halve the fruit then give it a few taps to shake them out.

parsley

39

CHAPTER 7
PEPPING UP POTATOES

If you are like many people in the United States, you probably eat a lot of potatoes. Impress your friends by serving up this staple more creatively.

Be Inspired

New potatoes are young, small potatoes that are sweeter than fully grown ones. They need to simmer for a shorter time than large potatoes, often only ten minutes. They are tasty served warm, tossed in butter and chopped parsley leaves, or cool in a salad.

The simplest way to cook potatoes is to cut them in halves or quarters, and then cook in simmering water for twenty to twenty-five minutes. Other methods include mashing (see opposite), roasting in quarters or wedges (see page 44), or baking in a sauce (see page 42).

Switch It Up

Feel like a baked potato? Choose a large baking potato, scrub it clean, prick the skin with a fork a few times, then rub with a little olive oil and salt. Put the potato directly on the oven shelf and bake at 390°F (200°C) for sixty to eighty minutes. Serve with grated cheese, sour cream, baked beans, or slaw.

Mastering the Basics
Mashed Potatoes

Mashed potatoes are a fabulous comfort food, but how do you make ones that are not lumpy or slushy? Here is how:

1. You will need about 2 lb (900 g) of potatoes for four people. Use a potato peeler to remove the skins as thinly as possible, then cut the potatoes into evenly sized pieces. If they are large potatoes, quarter them; if they are smaller, halve them. Wash the potato pieces under running water.
2. Place the potatoes in a saucepan, then pour in enough cold water to cover. Add 1 tsp salt to raise the boiling temperature of the water so your potatoes cook really well.
3. Over a high heat, bring the water to a vigorous boil. Now turn down the heat so the water is boiling more gently. Cover the pan with a lid and boil for twenty to twenty-five minutes. Check if your potatoes are ready by piercing them with a skewer or knife in the center—they should not feel hard.
4. Drain your potatoes carefully by placing a large colander in the sink, then tipping them in.
5. Put the potatoes back in the pan, then add 2 oz (55 g) butter, 6 tbsp of hot milk, and salt and pepper to season.
6. Mash thoroughly with a vegetable masher until smooth.

DAUPHINOISE POTATOES

If you master this classic side dish, you will feel as if you are in a fancy French restaurant.

You Will Need
- 1 lb (450 g) potatoes, such as Yukon Gold
- 1 cup (240 ml) heavy cream
- 1 cup (240 ml) milk
- 2 garlic cloves, peeled
- 2 oz (55 g) Gruyère or other hard cheese, grated

Instructions
1. Preheat the oven to 370°F (190°C).
2. Peel and wash the potatoes, then slice them very finely, around $\frac{1}{8}$ inch (3–4 mm) thick.
3. Put the cream, milk, and garlic cloves into a large saucepan and bring to a simmer.
4. Add the potatoes to the cream, then simmer for three minutes, stirring to keep the potatoes from sticking to one another or to the pan.
5. Remove the potatoes using a slotted spoon, then layer them about 2 inches (5 cm) deep in a large ovenproof dish.
6. Remove the garlic cloves from the cream, then pour the cream over the potatoes.
7. Sprinkle with the cheese, then bake for thirty to thirty-five minutes, until the potatoes are soft and browned.

A cheesy, crispy classic!

Gruyère cheese

CHEF'S TIP
For a rich, restaurant-ready taste, add ¼ tsp of grated nutmeg to the cheese.

43

SPICY POTATO WEDGES

These baked beauties are a healthier option than French fries—but no less delicious.

Serve with a splash of sour cream.

You Will Need
1 lb (450 g) potatoes, such as Yukon Gold
2 tbsp olive oil
2 tsp paprika
Salt and pepper

Instructions
1. Preheat your oven to 390°F (200°C).
2. For fiber-rich, skin-on wedges, scrub your potatoes with a brush until they are clean. Cut away any gnarled "eyes" in the potatoes.
3. Cut the potatoes into thick wedges, about 1 inch (2.5 cm) thick on the outside edge.
4. Bring a large pan of water to a boil. Add your wedges, then boil for eight to ten minutes.
5. Drain your potatoes in a colander.
6. In a large bowl, coat the wedges in a mixture of olive oil, paprika, salt, and pepper. Make sure the wedges are thoroughly covered.
7. Spread the wedges on a baking sheet, then bake for thirty minutes, until they are crispy on the outside.

CHEF'S TIP
If you like your food spicy, sprinkle over 2 tsp of chili powder before baking.

GLOSSARY

boiling When a liquid is so hot that it releases large bubbles of gas.

bulgur wheat The kernels of durum wheat, a very hard variety of wheat.

carbohydrates Food molecules contained in starchy foods, such as pasta, grains, and potatoes, as well as sugars and fibers, which provide most of your energy.

couscous Tiny balls of durum wheat, a very hard variety of wheat.

fiber Long molecules that are contained in plants and help with digestion.

fry Cook in hot oil or another kind of fat.

garlic cloves The individual sections of a bulb of garlic.

gluten A mixture of two proteins found in cereal grains such as wheat, barley, rye, and some oats.

intolerance An inability to eat a food without having side effects.

marinade A mixture of spices and other ingredients in which food is soaked before cooking to flavor or soften it.

nutrient A substance found in food that provides essential nourishment for health and growth.

protein A substance found in lentils, beans, nuts, seeds, meat, fish, eggs, and dairy products that is essential for growth and health.

pulses The seeds of food crops in the legume family, such as peas, beans, and lentils.

rennet A product made in the stomach of a calf or other young animal.

roasting Cooking food in the heat of an oven.

saturated fat A type of "unhealthy" fat that is usually found in animal products such as meat and dairy.

simmered Heated enough to bubble gently but not to boil.

staple A food that makes up a large part of a region's diet.

tempeh An Indonesian dish made from fermented soybeans.

tofu A soft, pale-colored food made from curdled soy milk.

vegan A person who does not eat any animal products, including eggs, milk products, and honey.

whole grains Grains obtained from cereal crops, such as wheat, that have not had their germ (kernel) and bran (outer layer) removed.

FURTHER READING

Books

Deering, Alison. *Hold the Meat: Vegetarian Sandwiches for Kids*. North Mankato, MN: Capstone Press, 2017.

Federman, Carolyn. *New Favorites for New Cooks*. Berkeley, CA: Ten Speed Press, 2018.

Hughes, Meredith Sayles. *Plants vs. Meats: The Health, History, and Ethics of What We Eat*. Minneapolis, MN: Twenty-First Century Books, 2016.

Warren, Rachel Meltzer. *The Smart Girl's Guide to Going Vegetarian*. Naperville, IL: Sourcebooks Fire, 2014.

Websites

Becoming a Vegetarian
kidshealth.org/en/teens/vegetarian.html
Discover more about vegetarianism, health, and nutrition.

Menu Ideas for Vegetarian Teens
www.eatright.org/resource/food/nutrition/vegetarian-and-special-diets/menu-ideas-for-vegetarian-teens
This site has tips for finding recipes and an example menu.

Vegetarian Recipes
www.foodnetwork.com/topics/vegetarian-recipes
Discover more vegetarian recipes.

Publisher's note to educators and parents: Our editors have carefully reviewed these websites to ensure that they are suitable for students. Many websites change frequently, however, and we cannot guarantee that a site's future contents will continue to meet our high standards of quality and educational value. Be advised that students should be closely supervised whenever they access the Internet.

INDEX

carbohydrates 6, 8, 28
Chef's Tip 8, 13, 19, 21, 25, 27, 31, 33, 37, 39, 43, 45
cleanliness 9
cooking methods 10
dietary needs, special 5
fats 4
health 4–5, 16, 44
ingredients
  beans 5, 16, 20
  bell peppers 12, 27, 37
  bread 9, 14, 35
  broccoli 25
  bulgur wheat 8, 9, 34, 38
  butter 14, 31, 40, 41
  cabbage 20
  canola oil 27
  carrots 20, 37
  cauliflower 14
  cheese 5, 7, 8, 12, 14, 20, 31, 40, 42, 43
  couscous 9, 34, 35, 37
    cooking 35
  cream, heavy 42
  croutons 8
  eggplants 11
  eggs 6, 7, 16, 33
  flour 14, 17, 34
  garlic 19, 20, 25, 31, 37, 42
  grains 4, 5, 9, 14, 16, 34–39
    whole 4, 5, 9, 14, 16, 35
  herbs and spices 5, 8, 15, 19, 25, 37, 38, 40, 43, 45
    basil 37
    cayenne pepper 8
    chili 8, 45
    cinnamon 37
    cumin 37
    ginger 25
    mint leaves 8, 38

    mustard, English 15
    nutmeg 43
    paprika 19, 45
    parsley 19, 38, 40
    sage leaves 19
  hoisin sauce 27
  lemon juice 29, 38
  lime juice 27
  milk 6, 14, 41, 42
  mushrooms 13, 17, 18–19, 25, 27
  noodles 9
  nuts 16
  olive oil 5, 12, 19, 20, 31, 37, 38, 45
  olives 12
  onions 12, 13, 17, 19, 20, 25, 27, 38
  pasta 9
  peas 29, 33
  pepper 12, 14, 19, 20, 38, 41, 45
  polenta 35
  pomegranate 39
  potatoes 6, 40–45
    cooking 40, 41
  quinoa 16, 17
  rice 6, 8, 12, 28–33, 34, 35
    cooking 29
  salt 12, 14, 19, 20, 29, 37, 38, 41, 45
  scallions 33, 37
  seeds 16, 17, 25, 34
  sesame oil 25, 33
  shallots 31
  sour cream 7, 17, 18, 19, 40
  soy sauce 25, 27, 33
  tofu 5, 6, 16, 22–27
  tomatoes 5, 11, 12, 20, 30, 31, 37, 38
  vegetable oil 5, 33, 37
  vegetable stock 19, 20, 21, 31
  zucchini 27, 29, 37
legumes 16

Mastering the Basics 11, 17, 23, 29, 35, 41
  couscous, cooking 35
  onions, chopping 11
  potatoes, mashing 41
  rice, cooking 29
  sauces, thickening 17
  tofu, pressing 23
measurements 7
nutrients 4–5, 6, 13, 16–21, 22, 28, 33
  calcium 5
  fiber 28, 33
  iron 5, 22
  protein 4, 6, 13, 16–21, 22, 33
  vitamin B12 5
  vitamin D 5
pulses 16
recipes
  altering 8–9
  Bean Hotpot 10, 20–21
  Cauliflower and Cheese 10, 14–15
  Chinese Stir-Fry 24–25
  Dauphinoise Potatoes 42–43
  Egg-Fried Rice 32–33
  Mushroom Stroganoff 17, 18–19
  risotto 29
  Risotto al Pomodoro 30–31
  Spiced Couscous 36–37
  Spicy Potato Wedges 44–45
  Stuffed Bell Peppers 10, 11, 12–13
  Tabbouleh 38–39
  Tofu Kebabs 10, 26–27
Switch It Up 8, 17, 23, 29, 35, 40
vegan 4, 6, 7
vegetarian 4